I've Got A Little Black Book With My Poems In

By **Jonathan Paul Fear**

Author of **Fear Conquers All**

To my J

A lethal art
A ballet of controlled violence
It starts with a respectful bow
Then you unleash hell
Each move a controlled flow
Across the dojo
In a leap, a kick and a fist throw
An explosion of energy
Body moving in synergy
Taught to react and protect
Not attack or agitate
A lethal art
A ballet of controlled violence
Ends in a respectful bow.

Published in the United Kingdom.

ISBN: 9798557521437

www.thefear.net

Facebook: fearconquersall
Twitter: @FearConquers
Instagram: @FearConquersAll
Email: jonathanfear77@gmail.com

Index:

Fair warning fine people. Some of the poems contain the F word.

A Little Black Book

I've got a little black book
With my poems in
I know that line isn't mine
I would have used more of the Pink Floyd song
But copyright infringement is a serious crime
However
 I *do* have a little black book
And the poems inside
Are mine
All mine

My Poems

I like my poems
I hope you do too
If you don't
There's nothing that you can do
You can't call the poetry police
And dob me in
They're just a collection of words
With the odd expletive thrown in
Come on now, it's hardly a sin
Just throw them in the - sink!
There you are
Proof if you needed it
Not everything has to rhyme
The line above
Is no poetry crime
I only put it in to take up some time
I like my poems
I hope you do too!

I

I'm a poet but didn't know it
Well, I did know it
I just couldn't show it
Didn't think anyone would want
To hear all my words
So I held them back
For years and years
I hid them away
No word attack
Now I've got loads
An absolute stack
Some are sensible
Some totally out of whack
I'm a poet
And I'm glad, at last, to show it

At Least I Know It

I'm a punk
I'm a poet
Sometimes a dickhead
At least I know it
Heart in the right place
But don't always show it
Ball apparently in my court
Don't know where to throw it
Got the seed
But nowhere to grow it
I don't try to fit in
If I did
I'd blow it
Because
I'm just a punk
And a poet

A Words Waterfall

The words come tumbling out of my mind
At a speed to behold
I don't always know where they come from
Some are quiet words
Some are quite bold
Some are in a rage
An unfettered fury
Some are kind
Or hilariously (?) funny!
Sometimes they make sense
But not all
They just keep on tumbling
A words waterfall

Blank

It's a blank piece of paper
And that's how it remains
No words to share
No stories
No wisdom
No dreams
Just a blank piece of paper
And that's how it remains
The story of a life not lived
The story of pain
Of every opportunity, left, none of them remain
Just a blank piece of paper
And that's how it remains
No need for ink
No truths to explain
I've nothing to tell
Just a blank piece of paper
And that's how it remains

You

"You don't write poems."
"Yes I bloody do."
"That can't be your job
You look like a yob
You've got a skinhead
And loads of tattoos."

Taking Shape

A circle
A square
A rhomboid
A hexagon
A triangle
A rectangle
This poem is really taking shape

Where?

Where have you been?
What time do you call this?
The reading started
At quarter past six
I'm not being funny
But you are late
It's so unfair
I've made everyone else wait
I'm only joking
Please sit down
Take off that frown
You've missed nothing
Just a poem about a clown
If you are quite ready
I'll make a start
And read my poems
My word art

Where – At Eight?

Where have you been?
You're bloody late
The reading started
At quarter past eight
You've missed my poems
On love and hate
I wouldn't mind
But they are fecking great
If I'd known you were coming
I'd have tried to wait
I'm sorry I'm so angry
You've got me in a state
Where exactly have you been?
You're bloody late!

Now Where Are You Going?

Where are you going?
Don't walk out
Is it the loo you are after?
There is one about
But please don't leave
Why not have a wee at the back?
You'll be alright
I have no doubt
Don't worry
You'll still hear me
I promise I'll shout
No one else will notice
There's no one else about
You're my only audience member
So PLEASE don't walk out

Mixed:

A rag bag of subjects, including one of my favourite poems, "**I'm ready for school now**."

The Rubik cube one is an exaggeration of a true story, I bought it to relax and did anything BUT relax me!

"**The final bow**" was written after a bottle of red wine and a listen to a Jonny Cash song called **Hurt**. It is another I'm told would make a good song. Feel free, when I say free, oh hang on, I've made that joke already!

Oh and "**New car delay**" was the first, and I would imagine the last, poem the salesman at BMW will ever get in response to a simple email to a customer saying there is a delay with the delivery of a new motor!

I'm Ready For School Now

A rubber
A pencil
A protractor
A pen
A paperclip and compass
My drawings
Some paper
A feather - I pretend it is from an eagle
A crayon - broken in two
Plus bubblegum
Shhh, I'm not meant to have sweets
I'll not be telling them – will you?
An elastic band - I love the twang and shooting it around
Two marbles, one a steelie
Some top trumps
Not the full set, they would not all fit
Into my batman pencil case
With the shiny silver zip
I'm ready now
For my first day at school

Rubik Relax

I bought a Rubik's cube
I thought it would relax me
I got one side all right
The side was all white
But then with a twist and turn
It all went wrong
And I couldn't get it back
To how it was meant to be
I bought a Rubik's cube
I thought it would relax me
My anger rose
And the cube was thrown
It rebounded off my wall
And hit me in the face
And down I did fall
Blood flowed
I'm a bloody disgrace
I bought a Rubik's cube
I thought it would relax me
Now I'm in casualty
Bits of the puzzle embedded deeply
I bought a Rubik's cube
It didn't relax me

Rock Star Meltdown

Rock star
Meltdown
Take the sniff
Clown around
Lonely life
Miss my wife
Still cheat though
Can't resist
Beautiful ladies
Under the sheets
Oh my God
I'm so pissed
Hotel room
After hotel room
Miles away
Only connection
Is the phone
Repetitive interviews
I'm all doom and gloom
Living for the moment
I climb on stage
Come alive
Crowd all rise
Music flows
After though
They go home
And once again
I'm all alone
Jack Daniels
My main friend
When the hell
Will this tour end?

The Final Bow

As the lights go out
And I leave the stage
One final bow
One final charade
The smile wearing thin
But no one can tell
The act almost complete
I've played it so well
The pain and despair covered
By the lights going out
From the crowd comes one final shout
They want it so badly
As far as I can tell
They all seem happy
I feel I'm in hell
But all they need
Is that final bow
As the lights go out
And I leave the stage
They go home happy
My spirit just fades
I won't be back
I've left the stage
With that last and final bow
My lights go out
As happens with age

Confessions Of An Angry Man

These are the confessions of an angry man
Long overdue
These are my confessions
Just for you
I'll list all my sins
Of which there are many
Everyone I damaged
Every soul I hurt
Every beating and knifing
All the blood that did spurt
The list will be endless
None of my transgressions were painless
My last confession
Is all I have left
I won't ask for forgiveness
None will be due
I confess it all
But no apology
Not to any of you
I've lived life
As an angry man
And here it ends
So screw it
And screw you

White Van Driver

I just want to be accepted
As I really am
An aggressive little bastard
Behind the wheel of a white van
I don't stop or indicate
That's just the way I am
An aggressive little bastard
Behind the wheel of a white van
I have no temper control
I'm a total asshole
An aggressive little bastard
Behind the wheel of a white van

Stand And Fight

Don't run
Turn and fight
No time for fright
Face them
Fists flying
Lip split, blood spraying
Hit them
Hit them harder
But then comes the first kick
And down you go
They carry on kicking
The kicks all around you flow
Lights out
You are done
How on earth
Did you not know
You *should* have run?

RUN

Run
Run
As fast as you can
Run faster
Run, man run
Because if they catch you
You will be done
So run
Run
As fast as you can
Run faster
Run man, run
Because if they catch you
You will be done
Run
Run
RUN

Hitman

I pulled the trigger
And lead flew out
Before he knew it
He stumbled and fell
A painful breath
A shocked yelp
Blood leaving his body
As was his life
Death once more delivered
With one pull
Of the hitman's trigger
A rifles justice
Once more dished out

A Mistake

You are about to make the biggest mistake of your life
I was not looking for a fight
But I will not back down
If you think I will run
Or you think I will fright
Think again
Be more polite
If not
With great gladness
I will punch out your lights
You should be looking to spread goodness
Be a good guy
Not referred to as vile
Spreading nothing but nastiness
Hatred and bile
Do not make the biggest mistake of your life

The King Of Social Media

I can amplify my words
No avoiding me now
You don't have the choice
Hear the words that I yell
I'm the king of social media
Share what I say
My 'wisdom' needs repeating
Or so I do claim
Dominating the airspace
Is my only aim
I am the king of social media
You will all know my name

The Origin Of Evil

The origin of evil
Has never been explained
Look on the tv
Or any newspaper page
The world is so angry
People full of rage
Fed by social media
And faux outrage
The origin of evil
May never be explained
But it looks to me, that evil
Could be in the final stage

Roaches

Roaches litter the room
Both the insects and the stub ends
Lowest of the low
Following the highest of highs
You must have missed the memo
"Just say no."
Chocking down the smoke
Then shooting up
And passing out
Colours flash before your eyes
The visions from a drugged up haze
It started as fun
It was just a phase
Now all fuelled by lies
End of times
Addiction has you in a prison
All of your own fruition
No life left
Just blurred lines and division
Horrors before the eyes
Are the only visions
As roaches litter your room

(For those that don't know, a roach is the remains of a joint, as well as the insect obviously)

Homeless

I'm soaked through
I'm freezing cold
I'm scared
I'm alone
No one to reach out to
No one to phone
No love to comfort
No shelter from the harsh winter sky
Disdain the only emotion
From the people who pass me by
They pretend not to see me
They'll not even look me in the eye
I'm soaked through
I'm freezing cold
I'm scared
I'm alone
If it could happen to me
It could happen to you
Maybe that's why you walk on by
And try not to view

I Still Didn't Run

3 v 1
that is no fun
I still didn't run
Not from anyone
Fists could have flown
But instead
There were none
3 v 1
Would have been no fun
Glad I did not run
But even more pleased
You all walked on!

I'm not

I'm not a violent man
But I live with a rage
It's ok for you
You can move on
Just turn the page

I try to control it
And keep it subdued
I try to fight away those damn blues
But you just keep on prodding
Provocation ensues

The fury wins out
You wanted this
Now we just scream and shout
Hurtful words
All you had to do was turn the damn page

Too Late

Tomorrow

Is

Too

Late

Don't

Stop

Don't

Wait

Don't

Wait

Shout

Now

Yell

Yell

Rebel

Rebel

Punk

Punk
where did the anger go?
Who
brought in the quite acceptance
does anyone know?
When
did the surrender occur
Whose
white flag did we raise?
Why
don't the youth fight and shout
Is
instragram the only thing there?
Punk
where did you go?
We
need you more now
Than
we all even know

Can't?

You are telling me you can't
Before you have even tried
So failure is guaranteed
Before your very eyes
Try the word can
And follow it with will
Put in some effort
You'll elevate your life
And things can be special
Stop hiding behind might
Get up and do it
Get up and fight
Learn to realise your dreams
Go to the extremes
Just don't give up
Before you've even tried
Get up - get out - live

Feeding The Soul

A million words bouncing around
Add some music
Boy, what a sound
Now add a screeching guitar
A drum, a bass
You've found the magic
A crowd you can control
Music is life
Music feeds the soul

A Lament To The Loss Of .3 Of A Mile

I'll never get back
That .3 of a mile
Too busy on a selfie
Peace sign and a smile
I walked on
GPS not set to play
Before I realised
And looked at the display
It should have said 9 miles
But 8.7 was the way
And now I'll never get back
That .3 of a mile
Much to my sadness
Much to my dismay!

6.5

6.5 – all the way round
Expensive bike
Worth every pound
A small Mount Everest
A major cycle
Thought I'd never do it
But that Sunday was vital
A puff and a pant
A load of pain
But that was all sound
Onward and further
Until I couldn't turn round
The jubilation, a shock indeed
My own Mount Everest
And pride abound

Sorry?

Sorry, not sorry
You must follow me
Do as I say
Not as I do
I'm celebrity
I am more important
Your worship feeds me
No hypocrisy
You stay at home
So I can go and party
So sorry
Not sorry
I'm celebrity

Insane?

Halloween is over
But the ghosts remain
Those haunted faces
Etched in pain
No one else can see them
How do I explain
That Halloween is over
But the ghosts remain?

No New Car Delay

I want my beautiful new car
the 69 plate
I don't like the delay
I don't want it to be late
My current car is running out of petrol
it won't get far
I don't want to fill it again
my wallet is empty, which is bizarre
So update the software
and give it a wash
give me a ring
and I'll be over in a rush
The beauty of that car
my excitement knows no bounds
So no more delays please
Bring it straight round

Don't Be Sick On Your Shoes

And the best advice
From his loving wife
As he got ready
For a boozy night
Was don't be sick on your shoes
Don't be sick on your brand new shoes

But as the night progressed
Too much beer and spirits to ingest
Despite his level best
What a night - what a mess
The daft sod was - sick on his shoes
He was sick on his brand new shoes

Despite the very best of advice
From his trouble and strife
More gin drunk than in his whole life
With beer and wine as well that night
He was sick on his shoes
He was sick on his brand new shoes

False

Is it all false
Or is it just the dawn?

Love and love Loss

A collection of poems about love, and loss, and goodness knows what.

I have no idea where most of these come from, you would imagine that my heart has been ripped out, shredded, run over and put back into my chest reading them. I can confirm, it has not.

My heart, oh my heart, my heart… has not been broken!

Or So It Seems

I don't get anyone to love
Or so it seems
Broken promises
Shattered dreams

Better

I wish I was better
I wish I wasn't blue
I wish I was worthy
Of a beautiful person like you

Breath

The virgin's breath scared him away
Now they all have families
Whilst all he has are memories
Of better days

Unrequited

You were my everything
I was your nothing

You Looked

You looked so beautiful
As you walked away
How did I not see this day coming?
How could I have been so blind?
You were so loving, and warm, and kind
To see you in all your beauty
As you walked away
Never again to be seen
This is a nightmare, it should have been a dream
My fault
My mistake
I wish you love, light and a happy life
How did I not hold on to you?
How did I not make you my wife?
You looked so beautiful
As you walked away
So slowly
Hand in hand
With him

There Are No Words

As I'm trying to write
There should be words
But I have no words
I'm lost for words
My pen isn't moving
The paper stays bare
No ink, or words, that should be there
Even though there are millions to choose from
I have no words to write down
If only I could
I would tell you outright
But I can't tell you what
I'm trying to say
To tell you the tale
Because I have no words
Drop the pen
This is a fail

She Left

She left
just went away
She left
where to - she didn't say
She left
no words to sway
She left
one bitter day
She left
Heartbroken - life grey
She left
just went away

Goodbye My Darling

I said goodbye my darling
To someone I'd never met
I felt totally heartbroken
Don't understand the feeling of regret
I'm so sorry
I'll always love you
But now - you have to go
Tears flowing
For what – in this life – I do not know

My Place In The Queue

I think I missed my place in the queue
I'm sure I was meant to be by the side of you
I missed many a chance
Well, at least one or two
But the surgeon interrupted my life view
Then isolation replaced the 'me and you'
Time heals the loneliness
No, I'm not blue
But damn it to hell
I lost my place in the queue

The Most Beautiful Girl In The World?

You must be the most beautiful girl in the world
Shame you're a bitch
So good looking
Heart and soul of a witch
Trying to walk away
But you give me that itch
You must be the most beautiful girl in the world
But on the outside only
Work on your inner self
And you'll never find yourself lonely
You've caught me in your spell
But this love is so phoney
You are the most beautiful girl in the world
I've fallen head over heels for you
I'm caught in the net you have woven
Damn it, I know it, my heart will end up broken
You are the most beautiful girl in the world

Teach Me

Teach me
I want to learn
I missed some lessons
It must be my turn
Don't leave me hanging
To just crash and burn
Teach me
Touch me
Love me
I want to learn
Because it's you
And your love
That I yearn
Your passion
Your Warmth
Your Love
I must earn

There Was

There was a party
I was stood outside
I looked through the window
I saw you
My heart grew with pride
I went to wave
I nearly came in
That was – until
You started kissing
Started kissing him
There was a party
The fun was all inside
As I stood there
Alone
Outside
And cried

She

She wasn't sure
But always said no
Tried to change her mind
But for operations I'd always go
Hoped she'd wait
But recovery was slow
A glimmer of hope
Out of hospital I know
To ask the question
But still she said no
She always said no

The Proposal

Your beautiful eyes
The window to your soul
Every time I look into them
My love for you
Grows more whole

You are my angel
My everything
You're a beauty to behold
Whenever I am by your side
My love for you grows

Our souls are entwined
You bring heaven to me
I love you, adore you, your love is so sweet
You are my angel
You make my life complete

I Know

I know you are in heaven
I know that you are safe
You were taken too young
It made my heart break
Such a waste of a lovely life
Forever remembered
Always missed
I have no doubt
By angels you have been kissed
So I know you are in heaven
And I know that you are safe
Sleep well
And I pray
You save me a place

The Great Danger

Love is loneliness
Love is danger
You see her on a street corner
She's just a stranger
But she's stolen your heart
She's a head re-arranger
Your life had been simple
Now it will spiral
You can't handle emotion
Or real love
You see a glint in her eye
And when she smiles
A cute dimple
You follow in the shadows
This love is not simple
Because, you, she must never see
Because your love is that of a stranger
To her, you're a hidden danger
If you tried to get close
She'd scream
"Stay away
Stay away from me"
The life of a stalker
Of a warped love
A love
That will never be

I realised too late

So I realise
What I didn't think I had
Might well just have been broken
Smashed up, finished
Something never to be spoken
I said I had no heart
But I realised too late
I had a heart
It was just broken
My heart
Oh my heart
My heart
It was just broken

One

One drunken night
I thought I might
I felt alright
But in the cold fearful light
The chance came
And the chance passed
I might have known
The chance
Would not last

I Don't Know

I don't know love
Forever a stranger it will be
I don't know love
It remains a mystery to me
I don't know love
I never found it
You see
And love
Well
Love never found me
I don't know love
It seems a fantasy
I didn't try to find love
And love
Didn't try to find me
I don't know love

You

You snore
You yell
You drive me mad
As well you know
I've packed my bags
But I can't go

You rant
You rave
You don't try to behave
You'll have me in an early grave
But I'm unpacking my bags
Why can't I just go?
Only you and I – will ever really know

I Don't Do Dancing

I said
"I don't do dancing."
So off she walked
I didn't offer her a drink
I didn't even offer to talk

I told my brother
In front of my sister-in-law
She went ballistic
She said 'you're a fool'
Us women talk in code
Didn't you know?

But I answered honestly
I don't do dancing,
It's just not my flow
Off in a taxi, on my way home
And because I don't do dancing
I went home alone

I Miss The Us

I miss the you
I miss the us
I miss the you and me
Holding hands
And cuddling on the bus
I miss the look you gave me
I miss you making a fuss
I miss the love
And I miss the lust
I wonder what became of you
What became of us
I miss you

You Turned Away

I wanted to know you were still there
I looked
I stopped and stared
You saw me
And turned away
My heart went from hope
To utter dismay
I wanted to know you were still there
I looked
I wanted you to see me
I wanted you to care
You saw me
And turned away

Lost – No, Never Found

For some
Love is lost
For me
Love was never found
I had a look
But there was no love around

Happy New What?

The clock tics
The clock tocs
The bells chime
The corks pop
The fireworks explode
The parties all go on
Loving couples in full flow
The night reaching
A magical crescendo
But you
Are still alone
Still alone

A Million Love Songs

I could write a million love songs
And I could write a million more
Just for you
You're my love
You're my life
You're my angel
You I simply adore
I could write a million love songs
And I could write a million more

Things Were Said

Things were said that night
Words that could never be unspoken
Hearts were broken
No flowers or other tokens
Could fix the hurt
The things that were said
The departure from your bed
The words, that could never be unspoken
All left chocked
The hearts
They couldn't be unbroken
Things were said that night

Oh no

Oh no,
The words came to me one night
The best introduction to a poem ever
"The Flowers Of Romance" are dead
Then I realise, only 'are dead' are my words
The rest, are from the genius that is John Lydon
His lyrics, stuck in my head
So now the flowers of romance
Are dead!
Or are they?

The Flowers Of Romance!!

The flowers of romance
Are dead
No longer by her side
No longer in her bed
Engagement ring
Thrown back
Hitting me squarely on my head
The split
The moment of dread
No more love songs to her
No more romance ahead
Engagement ring for sale
The flowers of romance
Are dead

The Rising

It rose
It was interested in you
I couldn't show it
It wasn't in view
I got a tape measure
To give it a review
Make sure it was suitable
Suitable for you
It rose
It was interested in you
It's yours if you want
But I'm not sure you do

If

If you are the English rose
What am I
A fucking thorn?

You the beauty
Me the scorn?

Your face timeless
Mine old and warn

You the life
Me the lack of soul

You the rock
Me the roll

You the direction
Me the lack of control

If you are the light
Then I'm not so bright

You are loved
I'm just about alright

If you are the day
Am I the night?

You are the English rose
What am I?

Introspective:

From love and loss, to lost and found!

Different subjects, some heavy, some positive and not all about my good self. I have regularly had to tell people when showing them my poems, some are just a play on words, some are from my heart and soul, but trust me, they are not always autobiographical.

Honest!

Oh, and I do so love The Final Call, on page 109. A few people have told me it would make a great song, if anyone wants to use it, feel free, when I say free... ahem!

A Wild Rose

I crushed a wild rose, in my hand
In my hand
The thorns cut deep
And the blood flowed fast
The pain decreasing
The numbness didn't last

I spread the crushed petals, on my bed
On my bed
The sheets, they ran red
Overflowing and red
Life slowly ebbing
The sadness is going

I crushed a wild rose, in my hand
In my hand
As the sheets ran red,
Nothing was said
The wild rose, will soon be dead
The wild rose was me.

The delicate,
Damaged,
Beautiful
Wilting
Wild rose….

Was me

Lost

I tried to cry
But tears ran dry
The irony wasn't lost
At no matter what cost
There was a lack of commotion
I just couldn't find an emotion
And so I will forever be
Lost

A Life Metaphor?

I have a towel
With many stripes
I count them when I'm bored

If was bright
I just might
Make that a life metaphor

But it really isn't
Anything bright
Nothing of the sort

It's just a towel
With many stripes
That I count - when I am bored

Locked Up

There's a room in my home
Where I keep all my favourite things
I keep them all locked up
Just like my dreams
No one can see them
For I will never show
They are *my* things, like *my* dreams
I keep them secret and close
Do they have value?
To you, probably, no
But for me they are priceless
And I'll never share
I keep them all locked up
Only I know they're there

.

I Was A Ghost

I was a ghost
No one could see me
You could have stood by my side
And still not known I was there
My face
Just a deathly stare
No feeling
No emotion
Or life force to share
I was a ghost

Whispered

The spirt voices whispered
"I don't even know if he is allowed in."
The voices then just faded
What have I been excluded from?
What brought about this shame?
Why am I not welcome?
What benefits if they had let me in?
Was I close to heaven?
Or was it a mirror of my sin?

The Fog Descends (Jumbled)

Jumbled the words my head in are
Brain with life aches
Extremes about these bring
Descends the fog ensues confusion
Pain and bring about pain the tiredness blues
Life enemy of fatigue my the
Strife nothing and trouble
End always ups flair these but
And then the clarity returns
Onwards I go, always on with the show
And now my words flow
Life with brain aches
What's coming next
You just never know

(The words are jumbled inside my head
Life with brain aches
Bring about these extremes
The fog descends, confusion ensues
Tiredness and pain bring about the blues
Fatigue, the enemy of my life
Nothing but trouble and strife
But these flair ups always end)

Busted

I'm broken
But not done
Hurting
But having fun
Ill
But not glum
Just doing
Whatever can be done
Living my truth
Not answerable
To anyone

The Mirror

I looked in a broken mirror
And I was whole
The mirror was fixed
And my reflection was in bits
Fell apart
The image split
I smashed the mirror
Now I can't see
Any reflections – at all
Nothing stares back at me

You

You are wrenching at my soul
A gaping black hole
Of this I have no control
A torturous hand
No line in the sand
No voice to shout
No real way out
The sinister realisation
The grip of despair
No breath
Panic fills the air
A surrender to the struggle
Where fear wins out
Death being dispensed
Of that, there is no doubt

Be You

I wanted to be someone else
I wanted to be liked
I wanted to be black
I wanted to be white
I wanted to be brown
I wanted a happy face
I wanted to act like a clown
I wanted to be sultry
I wanted to always wear a frown
I wanted to be gay
I wanted to be straight
I wanted to be non-binary
I wanted to put on weight
I wanted to be slim
I wanted to be ripped
I wanted to be oh so funny
I wanted to be great
I wanted to be grim
I wanted to live the outside life
I wanted to work within
I wanted to have hair
I wanted a cool stare
I wanted to be blonde
I wanted to be right
I wanted to be wrong
I wanted to sing - the best ever song
I wanted to be someone else
I wanted to be liked
And if only I had realised
All along you see
If I wanted to be liked
I didn't have to be something different
All I had to be was me

From

From the heart
From the soul
From the universe
From the lack of self-control
From the rock
From the roll
From the anger
From the chi
From the you
From the me
From the happy
From the sad
From the good
From the bad
From the sane
From the mad
From the punk
From the poet
He said he's sometimes a dickhead
At least he does know it
Because wherever it is from
It is from his life
It is from his experience
And from his fight
From his spirit
His light shines bright

Tightrope

I live on a tightrope
Trying not to fall
One missed step
Could end it all
Do I live life safe?
That would be no life at all
So I'll balance the tightrope
And laugh at it all
So what if I fail?
So what if I fall?
I'll have given life my best shot
That is no failure at all

Happy

I have to be happy
I have to be glad
When tears come to my eyes
They mustn't be sad
Live for the good times
Just get through the bad
Search for the moments
Where joy wins out
Live life well
Laugh and shout
Leave people in no doubt
Life is for living
Let the good times flow out

My life

My life
Trouble and strife
Pain and disappointments
Loads of doctors
And bloody appointments
But none of that
Will ever define me
It's top efforts
And laughs
You see
That will make up
MY life

You Cut In Deep

You cut in deep
Your talk was cheap
Your fees weren't though
For years I owed
You tipped me in
That was a sin
Money before health
You caused so much strife
You nearly cost me my life
You cut in deep
But one thing I know
You could never beat me
Not even close

What Are The Life Odds?

I rolled the dice
I lost
So I rolled again

Believe

I wanted to believe in something
Other than myself
But then I put me on a pedestal
And at last
I had something to worship

Die Living

When I die
I want to have lived every day
Without a litany of excuses
No quarter given
Get up
Get out
Live
No fucks left to give
No failures
No poor choices
Mission being accomplished
Struggles and all
I plan to stand proud
And give life my all

The Shaman

The Shaman started healing
A cacophony of sound
The spirits I could sense them
Their energy all around
The drum beats echoed
The chants grew in strength
Fire, cursing and explosions of supernatural lengths
The chiming vibrated
Through my head
Shaking the body to the core
The world forever changing
I'll never be the same
As the Shaman started healing

Take It

Take out my brain
See what remains
Take away my soul
Will I still be whole?
Take away my control
Let someone else take the role
Take out my heart
I don't use it anyway
Take away my energy
Let it drain away
Just don't take away my pain
It's the only part of me that is sane

It Wasn't To Be

I wanted a scan
I didn't want to wait
The delay wasn't of my making
I'm now at heaven's gate
Life will go on
But not for me
I wanted someone to listen
But it wasn't to be

No One

I am a no one
from nowhere
No one notices me
when I pass by
no one stops to stare
Nothing to impress you
Why should you even care?
I'm just a no one
From nowhere
No idea where I'm going
Or if I am seen
I'm a never was
Not even a has-been

Don't Tell Me

Don't tell me what you think you saw
Tell me what you've seen
Don't tell me what you think occurred
Tell me what has been
Don't keep everything hidden
Put it in full sight
What you think should be secret
Is probably all alright
Don't tell me what you think I should hear
Tell me what I need
Don't cover up those deep wounds
Let them all bleed

Kick

Kick the bin
Kick the bucket
Kick whatever you want
Just say fuck it
Kick the mirror
Watch it shatter
Kick the wall
What does it matter
Just kick it
And while your at it
Kick the habit
Ten quid a packet
What a racket
Kick the car
For not stopping
Kick the driver
See him dropping
Kick the anger
And kick the blues
Kick the me
And kick the you's
Kick out at life
But whatever you do
Don't let it kick back
Don't let life kick you

The Final Call

I'm sitting on the platform called purgatory
destination unknown.
Stripped of all earthly possessions
in front of me - two phones.
One labelled heaven
written by an angel's hand.
The other
with a label saying hell
scrawled in blood
as the devil demands.
I sit here
silently - in the dark
I am all alone.
Waiting to see which one will ring
Will the angels or the demons collect me?
Which direction will be my forever home?

I Can't

I drink
It hurts less
I drink
Settles my head
I drink
And nothing seems so dark
I drink
Poems flow
I drink
It's all clear I now
I drink
Social animal
But
I can't turn to drink

In Deep

Put the needle in
Sink it deep
Pump in the filth
Let the heroine inwardly seep
Drug takes grip
Mind starts to slip
Pain now gone
Reality also
Soul slowly fading
H is now in control
Master of every thought
Moral level, set to naught
No witty retort
H has you in its grip
Only one way
For this relationship
To end
And end it will
It will end you
Your future no longer in full view
H has your life
The life of a junkie
The grim reaper soon due

Are You Crazy

Are you fucking crazy?
I guess you must be
In my hour of need
Off you fucked
Not a single thought for me
No friendship
No love
Not even any loyalty
Such a lucky escape
This truly must be
What?
No, not for you
A lucky escape for me

I am

I am the God of kingdom come
And I will bring you fury and rage
Nothing can contain me
No man-made cage
You've brought about my wrath
Now what you've sewn
You'll reap
Bow down to my vengeance
Mankind
For your sins
You will all weep

Fame

I wanted to be discovered
For what I do not know
Famous for doing nothing
Star of a reality show
I've been on tv
Now watch my Instagram grow
No skills to talk of
But everyone flocks to see
The famous untalented person
That person is me

I wanted to be famous
But now I'm just sad
The press seemed to love me
Then the press turned bad
Now I'm forgotten
The fans have moved on
For the next famous,
untalented person
Where did I go wrong?

I wanted to be famous
I wanted to be loved
There's nothing I wouldn't do
Just to get attention,
My 15 minutes of fame
Every show I was offered
They laughed at me, I hid the pain
After all, that is the price of fame
Hello?
Can you even hear me?
Is this mic still on?

Bright Star

Bright star
Fading now
One-minute shooting
The next, shot
The passing of time
Bells soon to chime
No regrets
Life lived as best
A once bright star
Faded now

The Climb

Steep and rocks
Snow and shale
Sunshine and light
Then blows a gale

Step by step
Up we climb
Breath gets shorter
Spirts though, chime

The summit spotted
One last push
Snow makes way
For views so lush

The challenge completed
Then a friend states
We're up a mountain
The descent still awaits

Best day ever
Base camp reached
A proud achievement
One more complete
But fuck me
That was steep!

Welcome To No Pleasuredome

Welcome to the new world order
No hard lines
No real borders
Honesty replaced
Even the liars
Are no longer disgraced
They are voted for
Honesty has been displaced
Welcome to the new world
Of anger and disorder

Retired

I'm retired
Don't want to be re-hired
Time for a rest
Put my words to the test
A different life now the quest
Less money, but more success

It's not all about the cash
It's about living
A mountain or two I plan to be visiting
I'll sit amongst the trees
And talk to the birds
Heck, I might even talk to the bees

It's my time now
No more meetings
I'll be out walking
Silly jokes I'll be speaking
And a book of poems
Is on my list
I might even be in the pub
Going to get p…. a shandy!
I'll have the time, so that'll be handy

It's up to me
No bank do I owe
I'm retired
No more 9 to 5
Say goodbye work
Cheerio

Life Has To Be Won

It's got to be worth it
It's got to be fun
It's got to be the greatest thing
That I've ever done
Whatever I do
No time to relax
No time to wait
Life cannot be re-run
Life has to be won

Tributes:

One to my mom on her 80th.

One to my best mate on his 40th.

One I was asked to do by Aston Villa's legendary captain Dennis Mortimer, to read out at Ron Saunders funeral. For those not well versed in football, that honour would be like David Beckham asking a Manchester United fan to do a poem about Sir Alex Ferguson.

I had a bit of fun with one about UB40 and another their saxophonist Brian Travers, who is a great guy with so much life spirit.

Oh and an ode to my football team – and one to football itself.

Quite where the idea for one on Amy Winehouse came from, I am not sure, but I am rather fond of the poem. And the Jay Z one is based on a famous song by him, 99 Problems.

Mom

She was just a little Annie girl
She grew up to be my mom
And she is, without doubt, the best – ever - one

Over ramps her mini could go
Was I still in the back
She didn't know

Ribena and biscuits at 11
Rupert the bear on BBC One
When it ended, tears in my eyes, I start to cry
She hugged me and said "You're alright son, he'll soon be back on."

She can even make a tonka truck fly
Probably best not to mention that
Let's move along

Abba was her favourite band
Then along came bloody Tom
How many concerts did I take you to mom?
For me, it felt like a hundred and one

You see, she's my mom
She knows what is what
And how to love her sons

She was just a little Annie girl
And I'm proud to call her my mom

Happy 40th!

He's my bestest mate
We let penguins through gates
World's greatest steaks
Spiders catapulted into space
His jokes are often a disgrace
Although the hambush one is ace

Snot doesn't stop the highest of stakes
When it's time to sleep
He doesn't wait
Toilets are his favourite
But kerbsides are just as great

Up a mountain he climbed
Titties he did chase
We nearly died going up
Which would have been a waste

He's claret and blue through and through
Even through the rut
Meeting a Villa legend
From the photo I got cut

Not being funny but where's the hotel he declares
"I fucking hate you"
Followed by a puppy dog stares
Then we get lost in a multi story car park
And a 'oh sod it' sigh we both did share

He's a tip top bloke
The nicest you could meet
But we are men who don't give compliments
And this all sounds too sweet
So we'll finish with an insult
He's a ****… whoops, I meant
He's got smelly feet…

Ron Saunders

Ron Saunders
The manager of all managers
A legend of our time
He brought the Villa everything
We really touched the sky

Ron Saunders
A man amongst all men
If you did what he asked of you
He'd move heaven and earth to help
If you didn't stop and listen though
He'd have you out or shout!

Ron Saunders
When he returned to wave to us, v the Blades, a happy day
He looked up to the Holte End, with a tear in his eye, then gave us a knowing smile
Because he could see what he still meant to us
And that will never die
Our best ever manager, no competition, by a country mile

Because Ron Saunders
Was the manager of all managers
A man above all men
He brought the Villa family everything
Of that, there is no doubt
And that is why, with reverence and pride
his name we all still shout

So Ron Saunders
The Villa family send their love
The Villa family say goodbye
Ron Saunders, OUR manager and legend
Now a beloved Holteender in the sky

Heady Days

80/81
The famous season
When our claret and blue heroes
Fought their lion's hearts out
And the league was won

A magic team
The skills, the goals, the victories, the fun
The beating heart of Villa
The fans
Had their season in the sun

80/81
The famous season
OUR team of claret and blue heroes
Legends, each and every one
Led by the managers of all managers
The one, and only, Ron

The Mighty Claret & Blue

Enjoy the season
Of claret and blue
Enjoy the arguments
The agreements too
Enjoy the shots on target
Enjoy the goals
Marvel at just how fast
the football goes
Endure the misses
And the fluky so and so's

Enjoy the opponents
Don't forget to boo
Enjoy the selections
See what the players can do
Enjoy the magic goal
from a simple one two

Enjoy the highs
Enjoy the lows
Enjoy the wins
Enjoy the goals
Enjoy the ones that got away
Never forget
we'll get them back one day

Endure the misses
Enjoy the hits
When you see the streaker
ignore his worst bits
Enjoy the manager
The coaches too
Enjoy when the players
Run into view

Enjoy the sunshine
for the first few games
A month from now
Enjoy the rain
Enjoy the snow and driving sleet
It won't matter
With our opponents beat

For this is the season
The reason for me
To put on my colours
And support my team
The Champions we may not be
That is too true
But the greatest of all teams
Between me and you
Will always be in our hearts
And our minds too
Enjoy the season
With the mighty claret and blue

Football

It's round
It goes up
It goes down
Sometimes in nets
Sometimes kicked right out the ground
Up in the air
And across the pitch, no sound
Hit with the head
And sometimes thrown around
The world switches on
Just to watch this round ball
The national obsession
Known as football

UB40

In 78, some Brummie boys
Signed off and formed a band
There were all, but 1 in 10
And decided to present arms
From on the dole
To platinum
A debut to behold
The Brummie boys
With reggae souls
And great songs to share around
In 79, the Hare and Hounds
To launch their stunning sounds
What followed was, worldwide fame
120 million records sold
A labour of love
For our Brummie gang
No rivers left to cross
They travelled the world
To sing their song
And thrill each and every crowd
And then they got
A walkway star
Not before time
The reggae boys
From Birmingham
Forever our Brummie pride

Brian Travers

Brian Travers
A son of Birmingham
A real life gem
A sparky
A gentleman

Picks up a sax
And women melt
Reggie sounds
Soon belt out
UB40's guvnor, without a doubt

I've no regrets
He told me once
My bucket list is done
No matter the weather, or problems faced
He only sees the sun

Brian Travers
A real life gem
A reggie boy
A gentleman
Pride of Birmingham

Amy

Amy asked,
"What kind of fuckery is this?"
No one answered
Left alone
Fame, but no rest
Paparazzi hounding
Her constant test
She fell into an abyss
Being a pop idol
We all assumed
Would be bliss
But for dear Amy
The voice of a generation
Something was badly amiss

Just 21 Problems

Jay Z has 99 problems
I have 21
My list was longer
But unlike Jazzy
I've been working on them
Whilst he bitched and rapped
I've got some gone
Then I've done this poem
And he has his song
Ok, I admit it
Jay Z has won
But when it comes to problems
I have 21
I don't have a bitch
So she's not one

War:

These, I believe, speak for themselves. The futility of war, the loss of the brave soldiers, and the brave words from the politicians who don't have to face the battles.

Their Gods

May their Gods bless
The soldiers who sacrifice their lives
Because their bravery ensures
As they fight on foreign shores
Our freedoms endure
So may their Gods bless them
God bless them
May their Gods bless them
Bless them all

As A Brave Soldier Falls

As a brave soldier falls
A small part of his nation falls with him
As the life leaves his body
On the battlefield where he fell
He lies alone
He'll never again
Return home
As the brave soldier dies
A small part of his proud nation dies with him

Bravery A Hundred Miles Away

Your fight them on the beaches speeches
Were strong, noble and true
But you hid behind your words
Not a battlefield in view
Your sabre rattling
Didn't quite ring true
From an office a hundred miles away
Whilst the brave soldiers fought and died for you

Haunted

A haunted battlefield
The war long since done
No trace of all the suffering
The river of blood
Long ago run
No more battles
Left to be won
Just the haunted sighs
Of our brave young soldiers
Who lay injured
Abandoned to painfully die
Grieving widows and children
Left alone to cry

Gassed

Choking
Gasping
Wheezing
Done
Gassed
Eyes
Streaming
Filled
Lungs
Choking
Gasping
Wheezing
Done
A
Life
Wasted
No
Battle
Won
Choking
Gasping
Wheezing
Life
Gone

Politics

I did a degree in politics, the longer I studied it, the more ridiculous I realised it was, the more I realised I could not be involved and in fact, the angrier I got. These thoughts haven't softened over the years, sadly.

The Truth

Only the truth will imprison you
The lies will set you free
It's the new world order
A whole new society
Where the truth will hurt you
And the lies allow you to reign supreme
Rulers of the free world
Not an honest word to be heard or seen

Only

Only the lies
Will set you free
In Our Parliament
No time for truth
No place for honesty

.

The Mother Of All Messes

From the mother of all Parliaments
To the mother of all messes
Angry words, abuse and anger
Results in nothing but distresses

"Erosion of faith in politics"
You aren't joking
You've exiled your moderates
And showed democracy is choking

I pray for grown up politics
And our parliamentary system working
But I don't trust any of you
Your duties you have been shirking

Poets & Liars

Poets use words
Priests use prayers
Politicians use lies
Poets write prose
Priests write sermons
Politicians write bullshit
They are all the same
I suppose

Brexit

Brexit
Bitter exit
Fed on bullshit
The country split
Arguments spit
Views polarised
Repeating lines
I'm right – you're wrong
The rhetoric
Goes on and on
All the time
Trenches dug
No room for understanding
Zero middle ground
Or common interest
Can be found
It was no big issue
Before Parliament
Turned into
A circus of clowns

United?

United we should stand
Divided we remain
We don't look who to love
We look who to blame
The elite want us split
And we all oblige just the same
We tear ourselves apart
Whilst they see us all slide
You sit meekly and accept the pain
We never learn from history
The lessons are there to explain
United we should stand
Divided we remain

Shout

Shout
Shout
Squabble
Squabble
Like a witch's coven
It's all toil and trouble

Bitch
Bitch
Moan
Moan
Your constant arguing
Is a white noise, a drone

Hear
Hear
Order
Order
A disgrace to the country
We need a new world order

So
Shout
Shout
Squabble
Squabble
We'll all suffer
For the chaos
You offer

A Spoiled Election Paper

I can't vote for any of you
Hang your heads in shame
You won't care one bit
For me, it caused much pain
Whilst you bitch, argue and bullshit
You all look like clowns
So I won't vote for any of you
Nowhere to put my cross down

Bullshit And Bluster

My name's Boris
and my incompetence will see you dead

I have stupid hair
and a big fat head

I break the rules
that you must follow

My education was expensive
but my head is hollow

Stay alert
but not to my lies

I get richer
whilst the elderly dies

I don't care
I'm top of the tree

I'll just blame the scientists
you can't blame me

The Gates

There are no more gatekeepers
No social control
Authorities can't hold back
The tidal wave of anger
Hatred has become an art
In time
With this unchallenged fury
We'll rip ourselves
Totally apart
The rise of the right
The rise of the left
The rise of hatred
The future is not bright
Unless our children learn from our mistakes
And turn things around
More time for understanding
More centre ground

Red White and Blue

It's red
It's white
It's crossed
And it's blue

It's racist
It's nasty
It's aggressive
It's you

It's negative
It's hatred
It's perverted
It's true

The symbol of pride
You've taken it too.
To die for your country
Is brave, strong and true
To hate for a colour
Is stupid – that's you

You take no prisoners
Cause you have no pride
You point at the union
But in gangs you must hide

I hate you
Your brothers
I just hate you all
I pity your outlook
You won't rise
You'll fall

The World Is Burning

The world is burning
We've set it on fire
Near hells gate now
Temperatures rise higher
The children trying to save us
From climate deniers
The world is burning
We've set it on fire

The Haunting Poems From Fear Conquers All

This chapter has a collection of poems that I began writing over 30 years. Some were first used in my autobiography (available on amazon or via thefear.net) called Fear Conquers All. They were written in the early to mid 1990's and I have to be honest, once written, I couldn't read them for years. They evoked too many emotions – which I guess is a good sign, poetry and art should challenge our emotions. Some of the later ones were the fight back, more positivity, which a friend of mine pointed out I needed to do.

He was so right.

Reflections

The mirror reflects a stranger
A stranger who's been to hell
The mirror shows a shadow
Of someone he knew so well
A shadow of an achiever
Whose future was so fine
Now he's just a stranger
Who feels it's no longer his time

I Think

I think I'm dying
I don't know why
I feel like crying
My tears are dry
I've tried to release it
But it won't go
Ask all the right questions
But no one seems to know
The fear of an illness
With nowhere to go

He's Gone

He's gone
just sailed away
He's gone
couldn't face another day
He's gone
to a better place
He's gone
no more pain to face

I Tried

I tried to help once
I tried to be good
I tried to be friendly
And do things I should
Now the tables have turned
And all I have learned
Means nothing
My plans are covered
Like sea over sand
Spoilt by a raw dealer's hand

Fuck Off

Fuck off and leave me alone
I don't want to answer the phone
People at the door
I don't want to see anymore
Nightmares that continue each day
Pain in the way
I'm angry
I'm hurt
I'm alone
Don't tell me your lies
I can see behind your eyes
Your interest is your own
I don't want to see you
And handle it that way
The things I could say
Fuck off and leave me alone

Pain

When you wake up and the sun is high
But your heart is low
You see the horizon
But have nowhere to go
Then you have felt pain

Lost and alone
In a life of prisons
To hold back all your dreams
To lose all your visions
If this is how the world seems
Then you have felt pain

Yesterday's News

A moment of interest
Sandwiched by the TV pages
The later stages
Of a long lonely age
From youth to man
From health to despair
Who cares?
You're yesterday's news

Flick on the tv
For two minutes see me
Then continue with your tea
Don't listen to the story
The thoughts much too gory
Who cares?
You're yesterday's news

Miles

You're miles away
but in our thoughts
The bitter retorts
the lack of feeling
My senses reeling
how best to deal
When anger and hurt
are the only things I feel

Weird

You're weird, the drinks you swill, the drugs and ill
the music loud, stand out of a crowd,
To be an enigma, is that the aim or as it comes?
Opposite but direct, kind but dark
Stars, hedges, tears and pain
Outside is where you'll always be
They might respect you
But who will accept you?
You're weird

Dark Room

In that dark room they call depression
Your mind goes from friend
To a dangerous weapon
Everyone is looking
But will never see
How different
How distant
How desperate you'll be

Demons

There are demons inside my head
They come with me to bed.
They are wrenching at my soul
My thoughts now out of control
If they beat me I can only hope
They will leave me alone
Or is a lifetime of torture their goal?

The End?

When you come to the end
Will it start again?
Will you meet your God?
Do you want to?
Would he accept you?
Or give you a blast?
The future as hard as the past?
How long can the cycle last?

Lasers

Lasers in the past
Shine so bright
Excited at night
The dreams alright

Lasers in the present
Lights dim as a candle
So hard to handle
Why must the dreams dwindle?

Lasers in the future
The lights gone out
Too tired to shout
What was this nightmare all about?

The Silent Scream

The silent scream
The end of a dream
The tears are dry
But flood invisible from my eyes

You have to be strong
Done nothing wrong
And all day long
All you want to do is die

Tormenter

There's better luck round the corner
How many corners to turn?
How many dreams have to burn?
Does my mind have to churn?
These dark and deadly pains
My life locked in chains
Will I meet my maker or is it tormenter?
Will I find the keys to my freedom?
Or forever burn?

Surgeon's Knife

The surgeon's knife cut deeper this time
As if my illness was some sort of crime
Left to deal with the way I feel
No sense of hope, no sign of life
No friends
No family
And certainly no wife
Why wait and suffer?
What lessons to learn?
To carry on blindly
Where else can I turn?

The Ghost

There's a ghost
It stares back at me
A shadow of a self
Not what I expect to see
The life drained
No fun
No ecstasy
A skeleton stripped of flesh
Of what life was meant to be
Just a ghost
That stares back at me
Not dead quite yet
But may just as well be
There's a ghost
It stares back at me

You Tried

You tried to kill me
I even tried myself
You game me tablets
But did sod all else
You left me stranded
Life on a shelf
Through your lack of care
You destroyed my health
But you couldn't beat me
Nor could anyone else
I'm a hundred times stronger
My spirit is my wealth

Blank Canvas

I'm just starting
My canvas is clear
I can be what I want to be
The dreams are all here
Nothing can stop me
 Or stand in my way
The world is my playground
And I'll live every day
Then when I am older
And grown to a man
I'll see what's on offer
And take with both hands

Grand Design

There's a grand design for all of us
Some designs we don't like
Not all will be film stars
Or ride Harley bikes
For some will drive taxis
And others will bake
Some will be builders
And grafters who make
Some will be teachers
Whilst others work nights
But I'll do my own designing
And be what I like

My Stay

I've decided I'm staying
I'm not going for you
Throw what you want at me
There's nothing you can do
You've just made me stronger
And harder to beat
I was on my knees
But I'm back on my feet
So throw what you want at me
For me there's no defeat
You thought that you had me
My surrender complete
But I'm back up and fighting
And one thing is true
I said I'd keep fighting
And my fight is with you

I've decided

I've decided I'm staying
I'm happy to say
You've thrown what you can at me
Now just go away
You can do what you want to
I don't care a jot
You only have one life
And this is my shot
It might not be perfect
That is just fact
But I say what goes now
You're not taking it back
So you just keep pushing
I'm pushing right back
Might not end the winner
But at least I can say
Life is for living
And I've lived every day

Journey

I said I would go there
So there I must go
My *final* destination
Not even I know
For life is a journey
Some parts are real fast
And some oh so slow
I'll just keep on travelling
Just go with the flow
And when I arrive there
At least I will know
I've completed my *journey*
And my strength will grow

Journey 2

I said I would go there
So go there I must
I'll travel with vigour
And head there with lust
I'll follow life's journey
The best that I can
And when I arrive there
I'll smile and just say
I've followed life's journey
From boy through to man

A Life Warrior

A life warrior
I've fought them all
In battle after battle
I've tried to stand tall

Scarred and battered yes
But that is all
Never beaten
Not beaten at all

Battle after battle
I fought them all
And one by one
I watched them fall

Put The Needle In Deep

Put the needle deep into the spine
Remove the evil
Relieve the pain
Do it again, then again
The torture relieved
The life just the same
A shunt
A chance
All worth the pain
To restore
Set free
Put back in the game
A future
A re-birth
Sing 'I am the resurrection'
Put the needle deep into the spine
Damn
Life back just the same

I Was Lost

I was lost
Now I'm found
Life pushed me one way
I brought it back round
Good luck takes hard work
Bad luck just flows
But I'll keep on trying
Till my future glows
And I'll take it further
I'll go to extremes
I'll expel my nightmares
And realise my dreams

Wrestled

I have wrestled my demons
And sent them away
I want new horizons
And to see better days
Life may not be perfect
My illness seems set to stay
But now I go with the flow
Live life by the day
Because I've wrestled my demons
And they've gone away

Not What You Want

It's not what you want that counts
I'm a free spirit
An un-convention
I don't impose on you
So stop attempting my re-invention

I don't fit your ideals
I don't want to
Be the same as all the others?
No bloody thank you

It's ok to be different
An individual
Standing alone
Doesn't have to leave you as residual

I'll live as I want to
Put your imposing advice aside
A poets mind slowly dying?
Not here on my side

So I'll live as I want
No conventions, I'm free
I'll make my own choices
Just let me be
It's not what you want that counts...

It's My Life

It's not what I want
You might not understand
I refuse to be forced
I won't live to your demands
It's ok to be different
My ink is my brand
It's an armour that is under
It's my life
I'll make my stand

The Departed

I've lost them
They've departed
Flown away
We've all re-started
No more demons in my head
It's just me when I go to bed
A loss of anger, hurt and pain
The torture ended
They can't return
Not ever again
They can't return
My life regained

Forgiven

I've been forgiven
Now to let it all go
No looking backwards
It's forwards I will flow
I won't count the cost
The price has been paid
No profit in lamenting
It's a new life that's been made

Rebel

I'm just a rebel
Without a cause
I take the actions
Without a pause
I like reactions
I'll take applause
Because
I'm just a rebel
Without a cause

It's Your Problem

It's your problem
Not mine
I'm enjoying life
I'm fucking fine
You don't seem that happy
I'm sorry to say
So why should I fit in with you
Come what may?
It's your problem
I'll live life my fucking way!

Fuck It

Apologies for the language! If you don't like the F word, then I'd recommend you don't read these!

I pledge

I pledge allegiance
To sweet fa
Loyalty is a lovely construct
But it does not pay
Well it does for some
For me it's just one way
So I'll pledge allegiance
To sweet fa
Unless I find something to have faith in
One fine day

Fuck Fuck Fuck

I pledge allegiance to fuck all
Fuck it all
Fuck you all
No fucks will be given
No fucks at all
Fuck the illness
Fuck the falls
Fuck the needles
Fuck them all
Fuck the drugs
Actually, fuck it, give me more
Oh fuck it
Now I'm fucked up on drugs
And feel fuck all
Oh fuck it
Just fuck it all
No fucks left to be given
No fucks at all

Billy Fucking Connolly

Billy Connolly was right
If you've got the word fuck
You need fuck all else
Fucking great
Or fucking rank
Fuck right off
Or fucking thanks
I fucking will
I fucking won't
I fucking do
I fucking don't
No fucks shall be given
Not a single one
I could fucking well
Go on and on
With the word fuck in your vocabulary
You'll be fucking fine
Thank fuck for Billy Connolly
Thank you Billy
For a fucking great time

Crazy

Are you fucking crazy?
I guess you must be
You've got lovely chips
And covered them in gravy!

Thank you for reading!

If you are a publisher, or anyone wants to reproduce any of these poems, feel free to give me a shout @ jonathanfear77@gmail.com

If you know Billy Connolly, please send him my ode to him!

Oh and don't forget you can still buy my autobiography **Fear Conquers All** – on Amazon and direct on thefear.net

Peace.

Read on for an extract from Fear Conquers All:

Prologue

As the specialist delivered the crushing news - "Sorry to say you've got Syringomyelia and you will require brain surgery." All I could say was, "Oh, so I'm not mad then?"

It was bizarre. Here I was with a highly respected brain specialist, sitting behind his massive desk, resplendent in his pin stripe suit and bow tie, telling me news that would crush most people and all I could feel was relief. I knew then that I could die but at least I wasn't doolally. I had suffered for over three years with symptoms that were growing increasingly painful and worrying, symptoms made light of to such an extent that I began to think I was taking leave of my senses.

It certainly couldn't have been described as the best news I've ever had, but at least the people who had doubted me for all that time could see that I had, in fact, been suffering from a very real and dangerous brain condition. It wasn't exactly vindication, but at least the people who'd implied it was 'all in my head' would realise that, yes, it was indeed 'all in my head', but not in the way they meant. I had been very strong to cope the way I did.

Actually, I'm kidding myself here - of course I had the right to feel vindicated. I was ill and had constantly been told there was nothing wrong with me. Quite what people thought I was playing at if there was nothing wrong, goodness only knows? It would have been nice to have been proved right with a slightly less extreme diagnosis mind you.

The doubters were many; whether they couldn't believe that someone so ill could carry on with such spirit I don't know. I can understand family and friends not realising the enormity of the problem, but I can't forgive the numerous (and I do mean numerous) health professionals who dismissed me without a second thought. Psychologically this was very hard to take - I was being told there was nothing wrong, when in fact I was quite literally dying.

I think it is fair to say that relief wasn't the reaction the specialist had expected or was used to! He wasn't exactly what I had expected from a brain surgeon either, especially as I was paying privately to see him.

In my experience, specialists usually behave slightly better to you when there is a cheque coming at the end of the consultation. That might sound bitter, but I have come up against some really hateful figures in the last 15 years. Private consultations usually mean that the specialists have a little bit more time to spend on you. I have waited for an appointment for more than three hours on several occasions only for the NHS doctor to spend five minutes with me. What a waste of time and resources.

However, at this appointment there was no respect or care shown to me at all. I have never trusted a man in a bow tie since that consultation. In fact, I sat there open-mouthed at the arrogance of the man. He didn't act as if what he was telling me was life-changing news.

Having spoken to other patients of his since, I certainly wasn't the only one to have been treated with such disdain; his skills definitely lay on the operating table and not in social interaction... I didn't require the diagnosis to be dressed up; I am a straight-talking, no-

nonsense type of person and I had already been passed from pillar to post throughout the life of this illness.

So all I wanted were the plain facts. But a little courtesy and respect would have been nice too.

I don't mind people with a cold or distant personality, but when a specialist throws a couple of leaflets at you, (one of which went flying onto the floor), utters a few words as if a life sentence has been passed and then expects the consultation to be over, it really takes the biscuit! Especially when you are told that the one leaflet, (an information sheet on a self-help group), was no longer up to date as the main contact had passed away due to Syringomyelia. You honestly couldn't script it, could you?

Medical professionals can't get emotionally involved because that would make their jobs impossible; however, they shouldn't act with such detachment when people's lives are on the line. They should realise their patients are often very scared, confused and worried. They don't have to break down in tears and say, "Poor you", but they can surely find it within themselves to show a bit of humanity and compassion. I believe the days of the specialists being viewed as little 'Gods' have long since passed; it's just no one has thought to tell them.

Having told me the name of the illness and the fact that I needed an operation, he considered his job done.

"I'm sorry, I have a few questions."

The response? A sigh. I had to refrain myself from having a few words - you have to bear in mind this man was going to go where no man had ever been before. Well not on me anyway.

I was dying (no pun intended) to say, "Oh my lord dear chap, am I keeping you from a pressing engagement? Shall I just leave and tell everyone it's okay, I've got a couple of leaflets?" I was also slightly pleased; at least the scans proved beyond doubt that I had a brain, something my teachers through the years had certainly doubted. I was relieved that I had taken someone with me to this consultation because, without my Dad for a witness, I don't think anyone would ever have believed the nature of what was to be a life-changing ten minutes.

I wanted to know - and I believed the questions to be perfectly reasonable and educated - what would happen if I didn't have the operation and what were the risks if I did have it? It appeared that there weren't any real options: you either take the surgical intervention or you can face paralysis and death, neither of which appealed to my 21-year-old self! At the very least, the crippling pains would have continued, and I simply could not function any longer with those symptoms, let alone the plethora of other problems that were presenting themselves.

I had known for some time that, whatever it was I was suffering from, was getting worse and this was later confirmed by the specialist. After the operation, he told my parents that he had only seen one other hind brain hernia as bad as mine.

However, during this consultation, when I pressed him about the risks, I certainly didn't expect him to answer in quite the way he did. He said, "Well, I haven't killed anyone since

1977. Some might say that is a good thing, others might say with the law of probability it could be you that updates that particular statistic."

Right. Thanks for that then, nice to end the chat on a high note. There's nothing like a bit of positive thinking and that was nothing like a bit of positive thinking! I dread to think how my mother would have reacted if she had been present - as she usually was. I think she would have simply passed out, hit the specialist or both.

Anyway, by the time I got to see this specialist, I felt so tired and was so ill that it certainly didn't come as a shock to me, nor did it unduly worry me. I have a very strange sense of humour and I seem to be able to detach myself from reality at times, (a trait that has kept me in good stead), although I've certainly had a few times when I've been physically and mentally stretched to the very limits.

If you can face up to these trials with a smile and a daft comment, I think you are far better prepared than the people who just crumble and moan. Then again if I had moaned more maybe the doctors would have listened to me before I reached crisis point? Sometimes I guess you can't win either way.

One of the great pities with this situation was that it wasn't just me that had to take all this on board and come to terms with it. I also had to see the reactions, the pain and the terrible levels of worry that it brought to my family and friends. It's strange when I broke the news to people, the most common reply I got was, "You're joking?"

Well, er, no. I never did quite see where the punch line to that particular 'joke' was but, as I was to learn over the years, people just don't know how to react to such extreme situations and they either shy away, or say the most ridiculous things to cover up their inability to cope.

My advice to anyone who find themselves in a similar situation is: if you don't know what to say, then instead of avoiding the issue, just be honest. There is no shame in admitting you feel awkward or that you don't know what to say. Just ask what you can do to help and remember it is the same person you knew before they developed an illness or problem. Surely that is better than being a coward and ostracising your friend or family member?

You'll also help to prevent leaving that person bitter, heartbroken or just plain lonely. I'm not sure that feeling of desertion ever fully goes away; I'd implore you not to inflict that on anyone, it's a horrendous thing to experience, believe me.

I remember coming home and breaking the news to Mom; I have always felt quite guilty because she was half way through her tea. You would think I could have waited for her to finish, but instead it all came out, and straight in the bin went the food. What a waste of a perfectly good roast chicken dinner. As I broke the news to friends, I found my dark sense of humour creeping in. I'd tell them I needed a brain operation and then say, "Well, when I say operation, I mean a brain search really." They might not have laughed, but I did.

The slightly spooky thing about this book is that I was told to write it at a spiritualist church! I had been to see the Bruce Willis film *The Sixth Sense* during which I sat and shivered throughout, and on the way home decided (for some reason, as I wasn't religious or particularly spiritual) to go and check when the next meeting was at a local spiritualist church.

I went to one and the couple who were holding the meeting came to me within minutes, saying they had a message. I was sceptical but also fascinated.

Anyway, having told me a few things about the here and now (some relating to me so closely I fail to see how they could have made it up), they then said the strongest message they were getting for me was to write the book. They were being told to pass the message on repeatedly. "Write the book. Write the book."

So here I am, writing the book. I just hope this is the bloody book they meant!

Journey

I said I would go there
So there I must go.
My final destination
Not even I know.
For life is a journey
Some fast and some slow.
I'll just keep on travelling
Just go with the flow.
And when I arrive there
At least I will know.
I've completed my journey
And my strength will grow.

Journey 2

I said I would go there
So go there I must
I'll travel with vigour
And head there with lust
I'll follow life's journey
The best that I can
And when I arrive there
I'll smile and just say
I've followed life's journey
From boy through to man.

The Journey

This isn't a book about being ill. This is a book that is meant to inspire. A book that shows no matter how much is thrown at you, you can still achieve great things.

This is my story. **Jonathan Fear - the story of a man who doesn't know the meaning of defeat**.

The book is about a physical, mental and spiritual journey. Going from death's door to the summit of Ben Nevis; from major operations to being featured in Men's Health 'Hero Edition'; from being rushed to A&E to competing in a marathon. And, I'm told, inspiring others along the way.

As the Men's Health article headline said: '***The story of a man who fought death, won and trained for the re-match.***'

The first part - '*I was born in a crossfire hurricane*' - covers the breakdown of a fit body and how I tried to deal with the total chaos my health and operations brought me.

You'll see I wasn't exactly an angel at school and what it's like being told there is nothing wrong with you, when there is something very seriously wrong. Throw in a NHS conspiracy and a host of major operations and we're done. Between this part of the book and the second, was a gap of ten years where I had to get back out 'there', re-claim my life and learn to control the chaos.

The second part - '*I am the storm*' - is all about taking control and rebuilding a life.

I'm a firm believer it isn't how many times you get knocked down in life; it's how many times you get back up. I aim to show you that's exactly what I've done. I hope it will inspire you.

Some of the subjects covered aren't the most cheerful; but I hope a fascinating insight into what happens when things go so very wrong and how I coped as my life slowly descended into the chaos from a chronic condition. And then the fightback!

Part one informs my life, part two defines it.

Fear Conquers All. Why? Read on and you'll find out.

I hope I can inspire you to Get up. Get out. Live.

Part One

I was born in a crossfire hurricane

(Credit: my beloved Rolling Stones - *Jumpin' Jack Flash*)

You Tried

You tried to kill me
I even tried myself.
You gave me tablets
But did sod all else.
You left me stranded
Life on a shelf.
Through your lack of care
You destroyed my health.
But you couldn't beat me
Nor could anyone else.
I'm a hundred times stronger
My spirit is my wealth.

1.

Nobody said life was meant to be easy

I've not heard a single philosopher, preacher, or great person of our time state that life was meant to be a breeze. These days though, people seem to think that it should be. The more we see others having a good time, the more we are convinced that life is easy for everyone else and that we are alone in our suffering. Total hog wash obviously. Perhaps we have all become part of the 'poor me generation' living our lives as victims instead of getting on with it. A whole generation who, instead of looking at what they have got, only see the things that they haven't.

The old saying, 'don't forget to smell the roses,' no matter how clichéd, is right. It doesn't matter how bad things get, there is always something positive or a 'nice moment' that can be focused on. I remember after I'd had one of my numerous rib operations, I was lying in the hospital bed and a sparrow hawk landed in a tree right by my window. I was in agony following a very painful procedure, but all that was forgotten for a few minutes while the hawk perched just ten feet or so away from me. I was spellbound. So, despite the fact I was in a horrible situation, there was still that enjoyable moment. If you miss these moments, then you miss out on life.

I'm afraid to say that no matter how much we would like things to be different, no one has a divine right to live on easy street. You just have to learn how to handle what life throws at you because it can easily turn into a constant stream of difficult decisions, problems, trials and tribulations.

It's up to us though, how we view what we have. The 'pint half-empty' people, I would assume, take far less enjoyment out of life than the optimistic 'half-full' fraternity. If you view everything as a negative, then life must surely just become a grind?

If you constantly think 'woe is me', then woe *will* be you. There are positives to be found in the most negative of times. You just need to look a bit harder to find them.

Life, as far as I can see, is about how you face up to your problems and deal with those challenges. Some people seem to have the ability to ride with the punches and come back for more. Others capitulate at the slightest provocation and spend the rest of their lives being the victim, blaming an event in their life for their failure to get back up and start again. I will say it again, it isn't how many times you get knocked down in life, it is how many times you get back up that counts.

It would be foolhardy to argue that even the most hardened amongst us don't have moments of self-doubt and lapse from their positive thinking. We all get frustrated, fed up or down right depressed. However, there are those that seem to enjoy and revel in woe and being negative. These people just baffle me. It appears some people actually quite like it; they appear to celebrate being seen as life's victims and it provides them with a constant stream of excuses as to why they can't do the things they say they want to.

It is far easier to use the tough breaks you get as an excuse and give up, point the finger at others and duck any responsibility at all. So instead of looking at ways to improve a situation, some just look at others and put their success down to luck; it can't be attributed to their hard work or them having the right attitude, it has to be down to the fact that 'they've had it easy'.

Want to read more?

Visit thefear.net or look for Fear Conquers All on Amazon.

Printed in Poland
by Amazon Fulfillment
Poland Sp. z o.o., Wrocław